# POISONING THE LAND

© Aladdin Books Ltd 1992

All rights reserved

*Designed and produced by*
Aladdin Books Ltd
28 Percy Street
London W1P 9FF

*First published in
Great Britain in 1992 by*
Franklin Watts Ltd
96 Leonard Street
London EC2A 4RH

ISBN 0 7496 0794 7

A CIP catalogue record for this book is available from the British Library.

Printed in Belgium

The publishers would like to acknowledge that the photographs reproduced within this book have been posed by models or have been obtained from photographic agencies.

| | |
|---|---|
| *Design* | David West Children's Book Design |
| *Designer* | Steve Woosnam-Savage |
| *Editors* | Michael Flaherty Yvonne Ibazebo |
| *Picture research* | Emma Krikler |
| *Illustrator* | Ian Moores |

*The author,* Martin Weitz, is a writer and award-winning television producer who specialises on health and environmental issues.

*The consultants:* Jacky Karas is a Senior Research Associate at the School of Envrionmental Sciences at the University of East Anglia.

Nigel Dudley is a senior researcher at Earth Resources Research, an environmental research organisation.

**SAVE OUR EARTH**

# POISONING THE LAND

**MARTIN WEITZ**

GLOUCESTER PRESS

# CONTENTS

IMPORTANCE OF THE LAND
6

AGRICULTURAL POLLUTION
8

USING THE LAND WISELY
10

MINING THE EARTH
12

BURIED POISONS
14

ON THE BEACH
16

AIRBORNE POLLUTION
18

RADIOACTIVE LAND
20

REPAIRING THE LAND
22

WHAT CAN BE DONE
24

WHAT YOU CAN DO
26

FACT FILES
28

GLOSSARY
31

INDEX
32

# INTRODUCTION

The land is very important to human beings, plants and animals. We build our homes, offices and factories on it and much of our water supply comes from groundwater. Plants get their food and water from the land, and herbivorous animals depend on these plants for food.

Over the last century, the various activities of mankind have poisoned large areas of land, destroying many habitats and killing off much of the wildlife. Repeated use of pesticides and artificial fertilizers destroy many useful soil organisms. These chemicals also pass into the food chain, causing health problems for animals and human beings. Poisonous gases released into the atmosphere from factories and car exhausts fall back on the land as acid rain.

Toxic wastes from industries and nuclear power plants are often buried within the ground. These burial sites are uninhabitable, and sometimes the buried chemicals leak into the ground and pollute the land and groundwater.

Industries and people are now looking for ways of reducing wastes, such as recycling and depending on less hazardous forms of energy. Some countries even have laws which regulate how much waste an industry may produce. These new developments should go some way in saving the land for future generations.

◀ A view of a nuclear test site in Nevada, USA. Areas where nuclear weapons are exploded or tested turn into radioactive wastelands. The land remains uninhabitable for thousands of years, and people who come into

# IMPORTANCE OF THE LAND

Land covers about one-third of the Earth's surface, and many plants rely directly on the land for food. Their roots absorb nourishing substances from the soil, such as phosphorus, sulphur and magnesium. These elements combine with carbon, oxygen and hydrogen to build the cells of the plants. Plants are also responsible for regulating the air we breathe. During photosynthesis, plants take in carbon dioxide and give out oxygen. All animals depend on the land in some way, including man.

Soil is made up of broken down rocks, water, air and the remains of dead plants and animals. Bacteria and fungi which live in soil help break down the dead plants and animals, adding important nutrients to the land. Other bacteria add substances like nitrogen to the soil, making it rich enough to support plant life.

Huge forests growing on the land act as homes to thousands of creatures. The rainforests in the tropics have existed for millions of years, and over half of the world's species of plants and animals live there. They provide medicines, food and wood for mankind.

**Soil is made up of two main layers – topsoil which contains organic matter and subsoil which contains minerals. Many animals make their home in the soil, including millions of earthworms and bacteria. These animals help to mix the nutrients as they burrow through soil. Plant roots grow deep into the soil. They help to keep it in place and prevent erosion.**

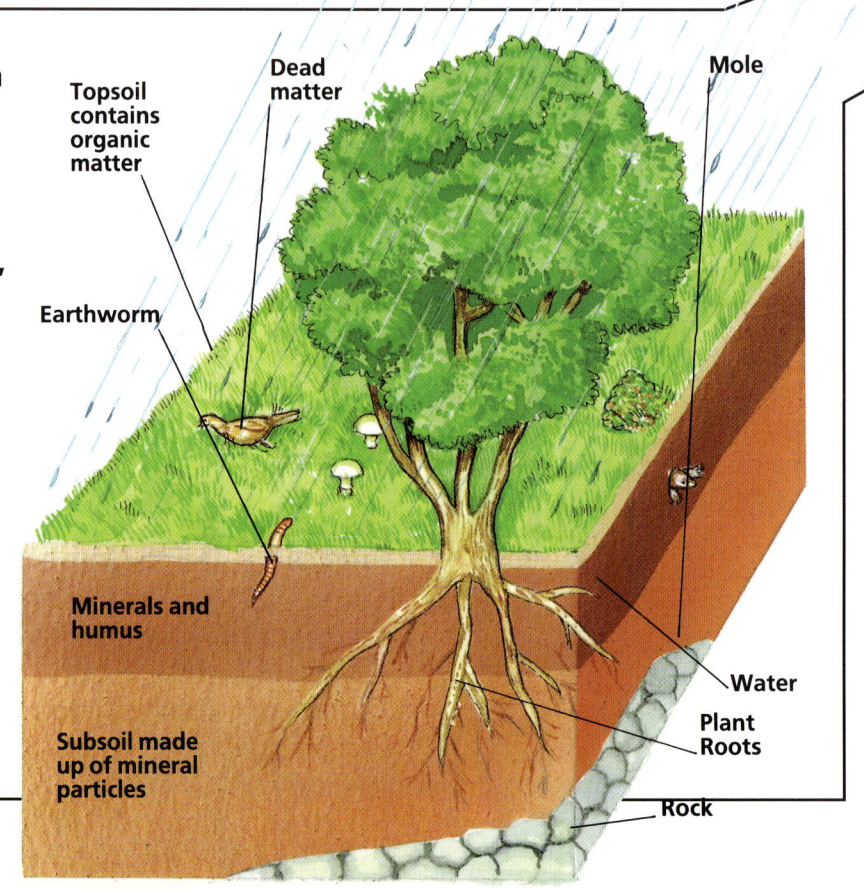

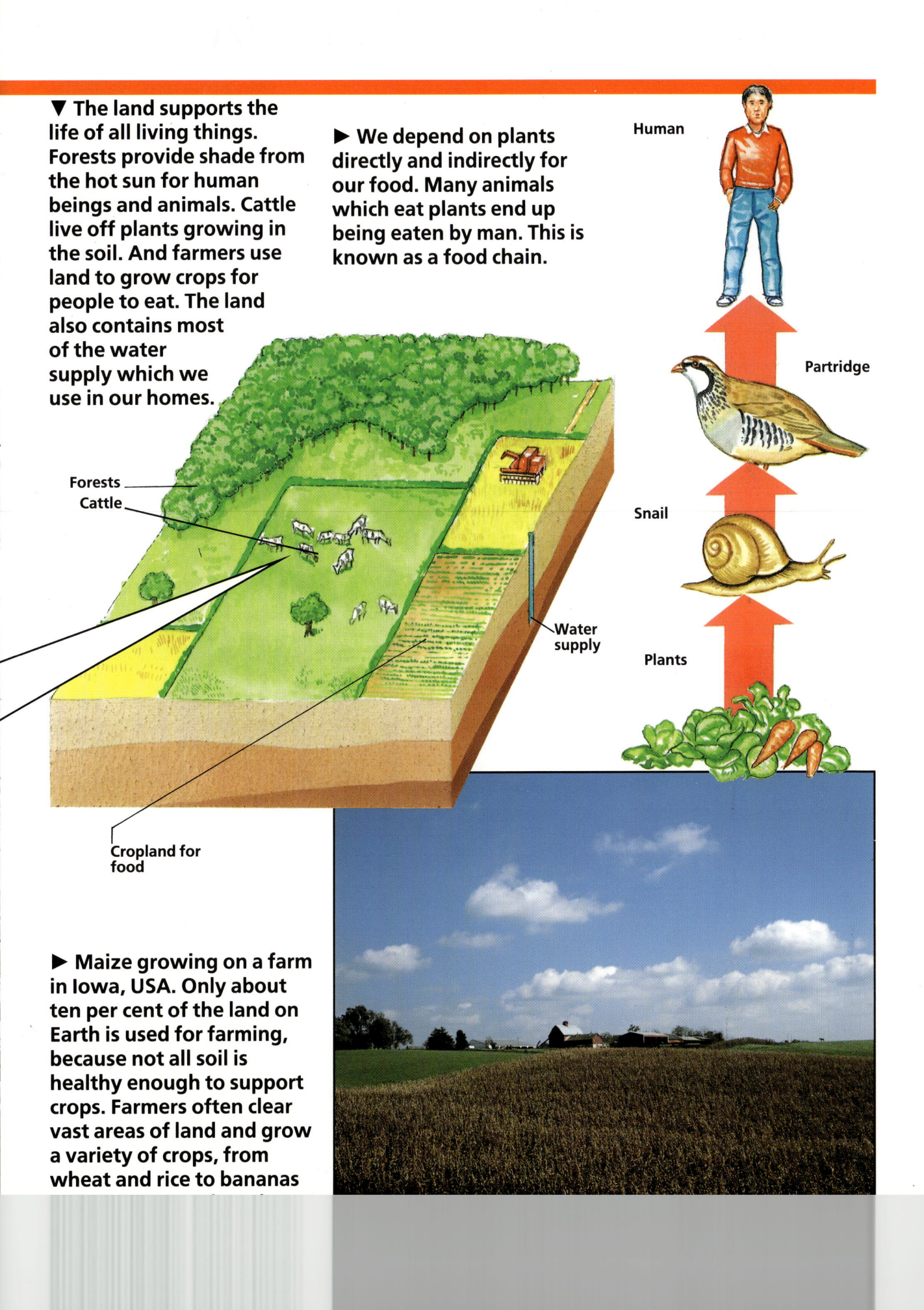

▼ The land supports the life of all living things. Forests provide shade from the hot sun for human beings and animals. Cattle live off plants growing in the soil. And farmers use land to grow crops for people to eat. The land also contains most of the water supply which we use in our homes.

► We depend on plants directly and indirectly for our food. Many animals which eat plants end up being eaten by man. This is known as a food chain.

Human

Partridge

Snail

Plants

Forests
Cattle
Water supply
Cropland for food

► Maize growing on a farm in Iowa, USA. Only about ten per cent of the land on Earth is used for farming, because not all soil is healthy enough to support crops. Farmers often clear vast areas of land and grow a variety of crops, from wheat and rice to bananas

# AGRICULTURAL POLLUTION

Although pesticides and fertilizers may give farmers a good yield of crops, they have an adverse effect on the land. Many pesticides are indiscriminate, killing off useful insects such as bees and butterflies, as well as harmful pests. Organophosphate pesticides such as carbofuran kill earthworms and other insects which are vital to a healthy soil. Insects also develop new, stronger breeds which can resist a particular pesticide.

Fertilizers disrupt the soil's natural cycle. Replacing compost and manure with liquid fertilizers reduces humus in topsoil which increases the risk of erosion. As the fertilizers get washed away, they leave the soil so unhealthy that a stronger concentration of fertilizer is needed to make crops grow on the land.

Clearing vast areas for farming also destroys the land. Trees and vegetation normally hold the soil in place and protect it from rain. Without them, the soil is easily blown away by the wind or washed away by rain. Topsoil is being lost at a rate of 25 million tonnes every year.

▼ **Pesticides which are sprayed on farms help to protect crops from harmful insects. But they also have damaging side effects, like weakening the soil and affecting animal health. High concentrations of pesticides also kill off bird life such as vultures, peregrine falcons and other birds of prey.**

▶ Most pesticides contain poisons which kill insects and other pests that harm crops. Fields sprayed with pesticides often have signs which warn people of the dangers. Herbicides, which are used to control weeds sometimes kill plants by attacking their messenger cells and stopping natural cell activity. Some pesticides have been linked with cancer in humans.

▲ Organic farmers use only natural pesticides and fertilizers to grow crops on their land. (1) Preparing grapes in a vineyard in ... land on a large organic farm in England. (3) Harvesting a vineyard in America's Nappa Valley. (4) Organically grown tomatoes on a

# USING THE LAND WISELY

One way of reducing pollution on land is by adopting organic farming methods. Instead of using artificial fertilizers, organic farmers grow such crops as clover and other legumes which add nitrogen to the soil. Organic farmers also make use of natural predators to control pests on their farms.

The land needs to be protected from the damaging effects of wind and rain. Planting trees helps hold the soil in place. Trees also provide shade from the scorching heat of the sun.

Growing plants with deep roots such as lucerne, acacia and comfrey helps the soil breathe. Raised beds prevent water logging, and rain is drained away without harming crops. Animals with hooves, such as cows and sheep, can damage soil. Their heavy hooves press the soil together and make it hard for plants to grow. To combat this, farmers need to reduce the number of animals or raise smaller ones such as chickens or geese.

**Planting date palms in Abu Dhabi. Farmers can turn once fertile lands into deserts and this process is known as desertification. Cutting down trees to grow crops, feeding too many livestock such as sheep, cattle and goats, on too little land contributes to desertification. Planting trees in the newly-formed deserts helps to stop it from spreading to other areas. This also protects crops from the harsh effects of the wind and rain. About 900 million hectares of land have already been turned into deserts over the last 50 years.**

▼ **Uncontrolled logging destroys habitats and ruins the land. The aerial view of Brazil's rainforest (left), shows the devastating effect deforestation has had on the land. Sensitive replanting schemes, such as the one at Wanchope forest (right), ensure that ravaged forests continue to provide timber, food and homes.**

▶ **Forests which have been ruined by commercial logging can be turned into farms or gardens. The forest garden shown on the right is in Devon, England. Growing crops such as beans or maize will help kill weeds and add nourishing substances, such as nitrogen, to the soil.**

# MINING THE EARTH

Mining is an ancient human activity. From mineral deposits we get such useful materials as coal, copper, iron, bauxite and uranium. These are used in many industries, from car manufacturing to producing energy in nuclear power plants.

But mining also destroys the land. Bulldozers dig up soil and vegetation so that power shovels can reach the minerals beneath the surface. Such land is hardly ever restored and may remain barren for years.

Sometimes the land above mines caves in or subsides, causing houses and roads to crack, railway tracks to bend and gas pipes to explode. The lead and zinc mines of Missouri and Oklahoma in the United States have made hundreds of homes collapse.

People who work in uranium, coal, tin and copper mines risk getting work-related diseases. Uranium miners are harmed by a gas called radon. It is produced by the uranium ore and can cause lung cancer.

On the Greek island of Thasos, crops grown close to old mining sites have been contaminated with heavy metals such as lead, zinc and manganese. The bauxite mines in Brazil have also polluted the surrounding soil.

▲ The effect of pollution from copper mines on trees in Australia. When copper is smelted, it releases poisonous gases such as sulphur dioxide into the atmosphere. The gases combine with water vapour in the atmosphere, and fall back as acid rain.

Different methods are used to extract minerals from the Earth. Minerals which lie deep within the ground, such as crude oil and natural gas, are extracted by subsurface mining. Minerals which lie close to the surface are extracted by surface mining. Several methods are used to mine minerals near the surface. For example, in open-pit mining large machines are used to remove minerals such as copper, iron and gravel. The open-pit copper mine on the left lies along the Peruvian coast. Most mines are not restored, and the land left without any vegetation is easily eroded.

# BURIED POISONS

Britain produces 5 million tonnes of poisonous waste every year, and 80 per cent of it is buried at special sites known as landfill sites. These wastes do not always stay buried. Some of them, such as solvents from the paint industry, can leak from their containers into the soil. Floods and earthquakes can also disturb buried wastes and allow them to pollute the land.

Often domestic and industrial wastes are buried together at these sites. In Britain, the sites receive an explosive cocktail of poisons – heavy metals such as mercury and cadmium found in products like batteries, pesticides, solvents, asbestos and PCBs (chemicals used in the electronics industry). Once these poisons get into the soil, they have devastating effects on plant and animal life. Crops contaminated with PCBs and cadmium pass the poisons down the food chain, causing cancer in human beings and animals.

In Holland, there are over 5,000 landfill sites and 350 of them are considered to be a threat to public health.

▼ **Scientists are trying to develop new kinds of bacteria that can degrade oil. Researchers hope the chemical-producing bacteria will be able to survive in the high temperatures and pressures of oil reservoirs. The bacterial chemicals will be used to lower the viscosity of oil and to clean up debris.**

◀ A dump of steel drums containing waste in Colorado, USA. Wastes from industries are sealed in containers and dumped at special sites. But the containers are never a hundred per cent safe, and some wastes end up seeping into the soil. The drums in this picture have not been labelled, and some of them may contain poisonous chemicals.

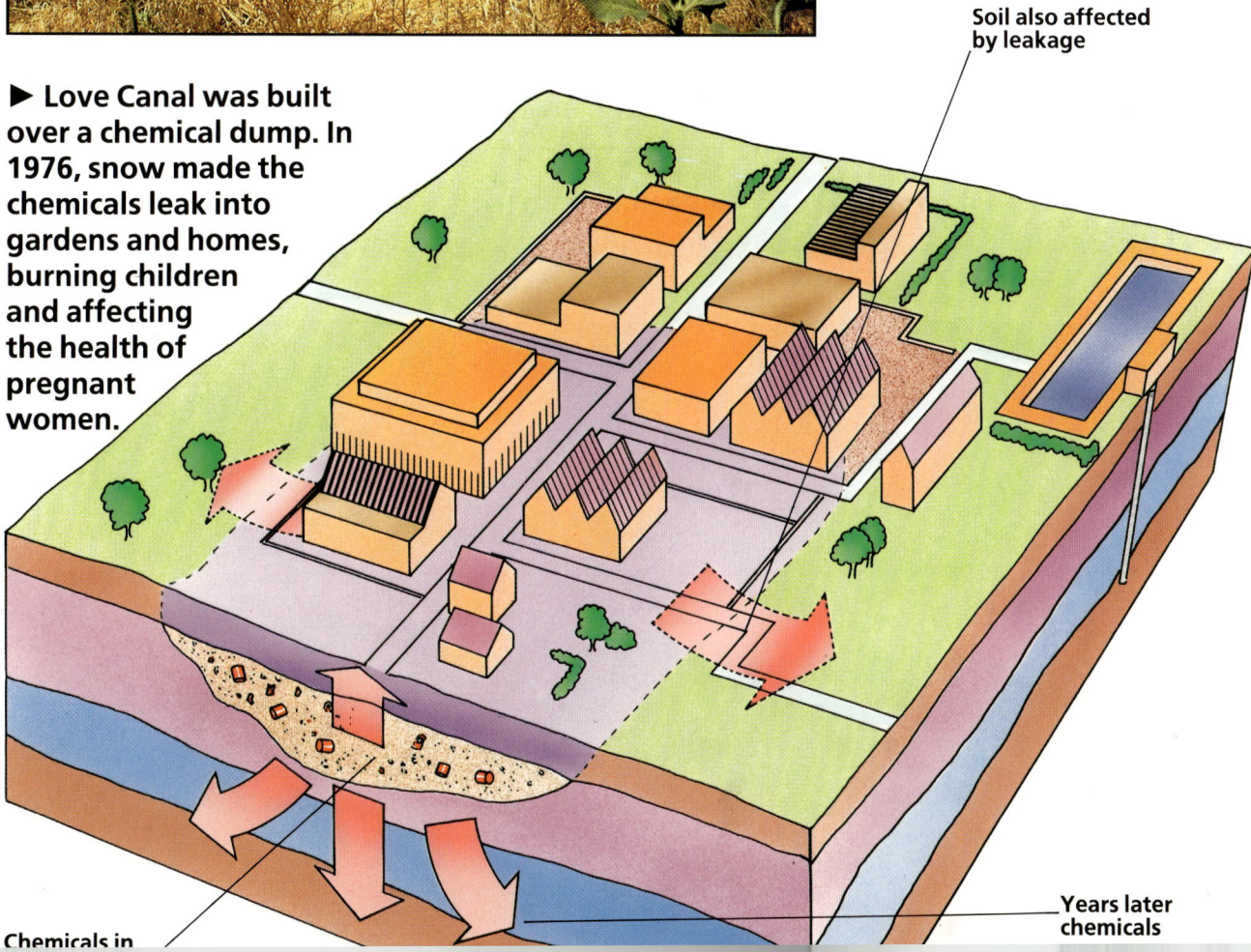

▶ Love Canal was built over a chemical dump. In 1976, snow made the chemicals leak into gardens and homes, burning children and affecting the health of pregnant women.

Soil also affected by leakage

Years later chemicals

Chemicals in

# ON THE BEACH

Many beaches around the world are polluted by both domestic and industrial wastes. Rubbish of all kinds – empty milk cartons, bottles, empty cans, plastic bags – end up along the beach. A lot of this litter is thrown into the sea by seamen out in the ocean. But some of it is left by people visiting the beaches.

In some coastal areas, untreated sewage dumped in the sea ends up getting washed up on beaches. Untreated sewage contains harmful bacteria and poisonous chemicals, such as bleaches and detergents. Swimmers run the risk of catching infections from the bacteria in sewage.

Other rubbish also ends up on the beach. Waste from hospitals such as syringes and blood samples have been found on beaches in America. Oil spilt far out at sea also washes up on the beach.

Sometimes drums containing poisonous chemicals are found along the beach. Some of them end up on the beach after accidents occur out in the ocean. Others are deliberately dumped at sea by countries that do not want to face the high cost of making them safe.

▼ A burning oil field in Kuwait. Spilt or burning oil causes a lot of damage to the environment. It destroys the land, leaving giant oil slicks. It kills marine and bird life. The poisonous fumes released by burning oil also pollute the atmosphere.

A beach in Hong Kong covered with domestic waste. Beaches like these are common in many parts of the world, and pose a danger to people and animals. The beaches are unsightly and can not be used by holiday makers. Also rotting rubbish produces a gas called methane. As it escapes into the environment, it damages the ozone layer. Methane trapped under piles of rubbish can also cause an explosion. Many plastics never break down but remain in rubbish tips for hundreds of years.

# AIRBORNE POLLUTION

The emission from power stations and factories contains harmful chemicals. As it rises into the atmosphere, wind carries it all over the land. In Britain, some of it ends up falling as acid rain in Sweden and Germany.

Another deadly chemical produced by industries is dioxin. Dioxins are produced when plastics and other products made from chlorine are burnt. If the dioxins fall on grass, they end up entering the food chain after cattle eat the contaminated grass. Dioxins affect the memory, muscles and nerves of unborn children. Even burning PVC plastics in gardens releases dioxins.

Petrol contains another dangerous product, lead. As cars drive along roads, lead from their exhaust pipes falls on the soil and is absorbed by plants. Lead can cause damage to the brain and nervous system.

▼ **Factories, power stations and cars all produce toxic substances. These pass into the atmosphere and are spread even further by the wind. The pollutants also combine with water vapour in the air to form sulphuric acid and nitric acid. These acids then fall back to the land, as acid rain.**

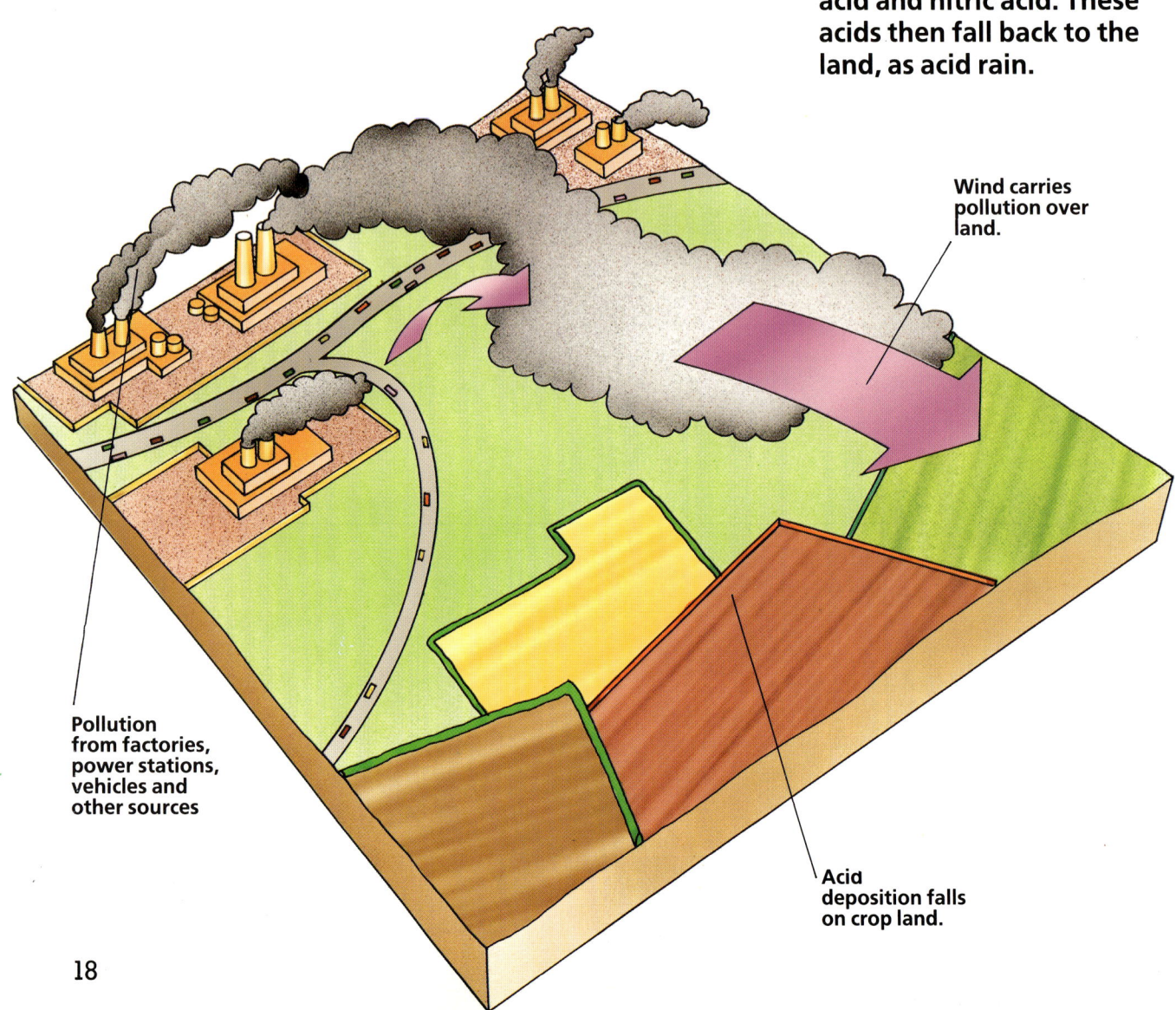

**Wind carries pollution over land.**

**Pollution from factories, power stations, vehicles and other sources**

**Acid deposition falls on crop land.**

▲ Contaminated tomatoes being dumped in a field in Italy. Pollution from man's activities often damages the soil, and ends up affecting crops. Crops which absorb the poisonous chemicals often have to be destroyed so that they do not affect the health of animals or man.

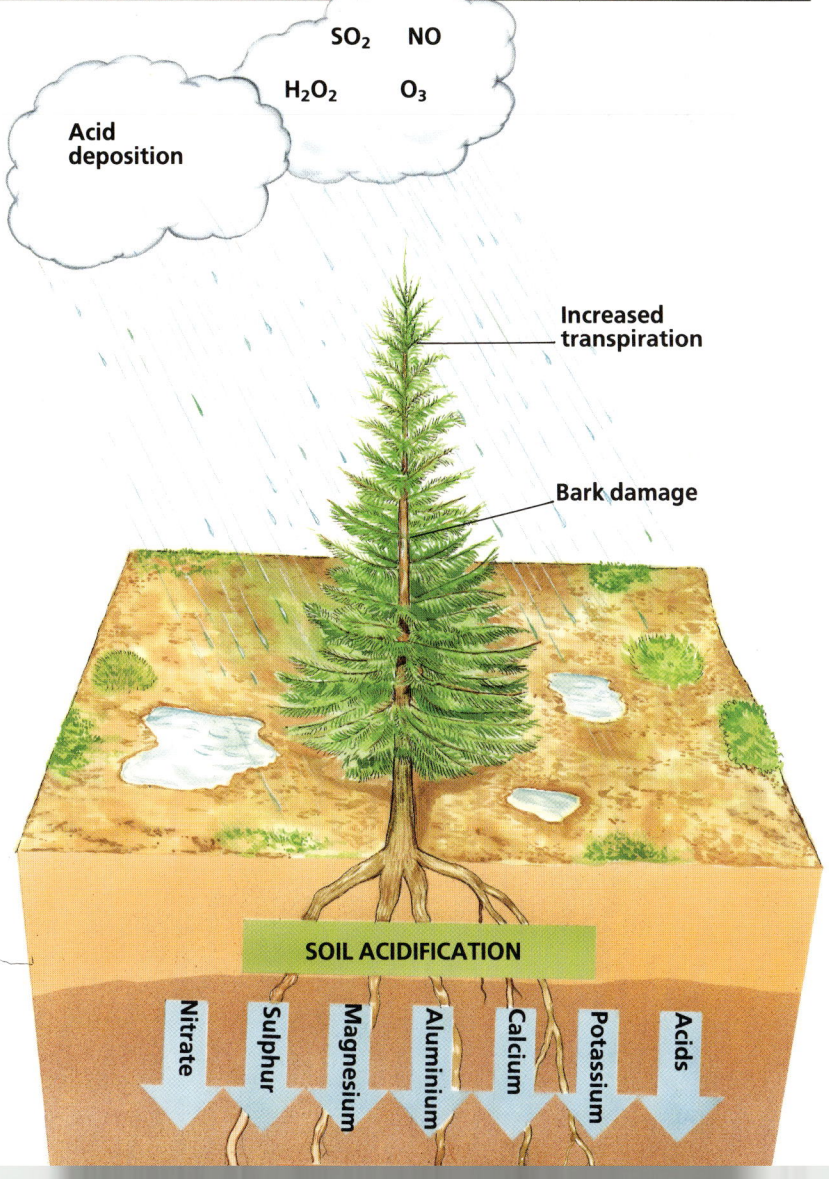

▶ Acid rain is a serious problem for plant life. Burning fossil fuels, such as coal, to heat homes or manufacture products, releases sulphur dioxide and nitrogen oxide into the atmosphere. These combine with water vapour in the air to form acids, which fall back to the land as rain or snow. When acid rain enters the soil, it

# RADIOACTIVE LAND

Uranium is used in nuclear reactors to produce electricity for our homes and factories. But mining uranium leaves vast areas of land radioactive for thousands of years. The debris from the mines, called tailings, emit a radioactive gas called radon-222. The tailings are often piled high on the ground close to mining sites or dumped in landfill sites. Some have even been used to construct homes and roads in America. High levels of radon gas in the environment have been linked with lung cancer in humans.

Another kind of radioactive pollution occurs when nuclear bombs are tested or when accidents happen at nuclear power plants. The poisonous radioactive fallout, or dust, is carried far and wide by the wind. It finally settles on the land, ruining the soil and destroying crops.

Some plants can even absorb radioactive substances through their roots. For example, caesium-137 is absorbed by grasses and plants because it resembles potassium, which is a vital nutrient for plants. After cows eat the radioactive grass, they pass the poison onto humans through their contaminated milk.

▼ **A nuclear waste storage site. The waste produced at nuclear power plants remains highly radioactive for thousands of years. Spent uranium rods used during nuclear fission are stored in pools of water near the site. After the rods have cooled down, they are transported to other sites for storage.**

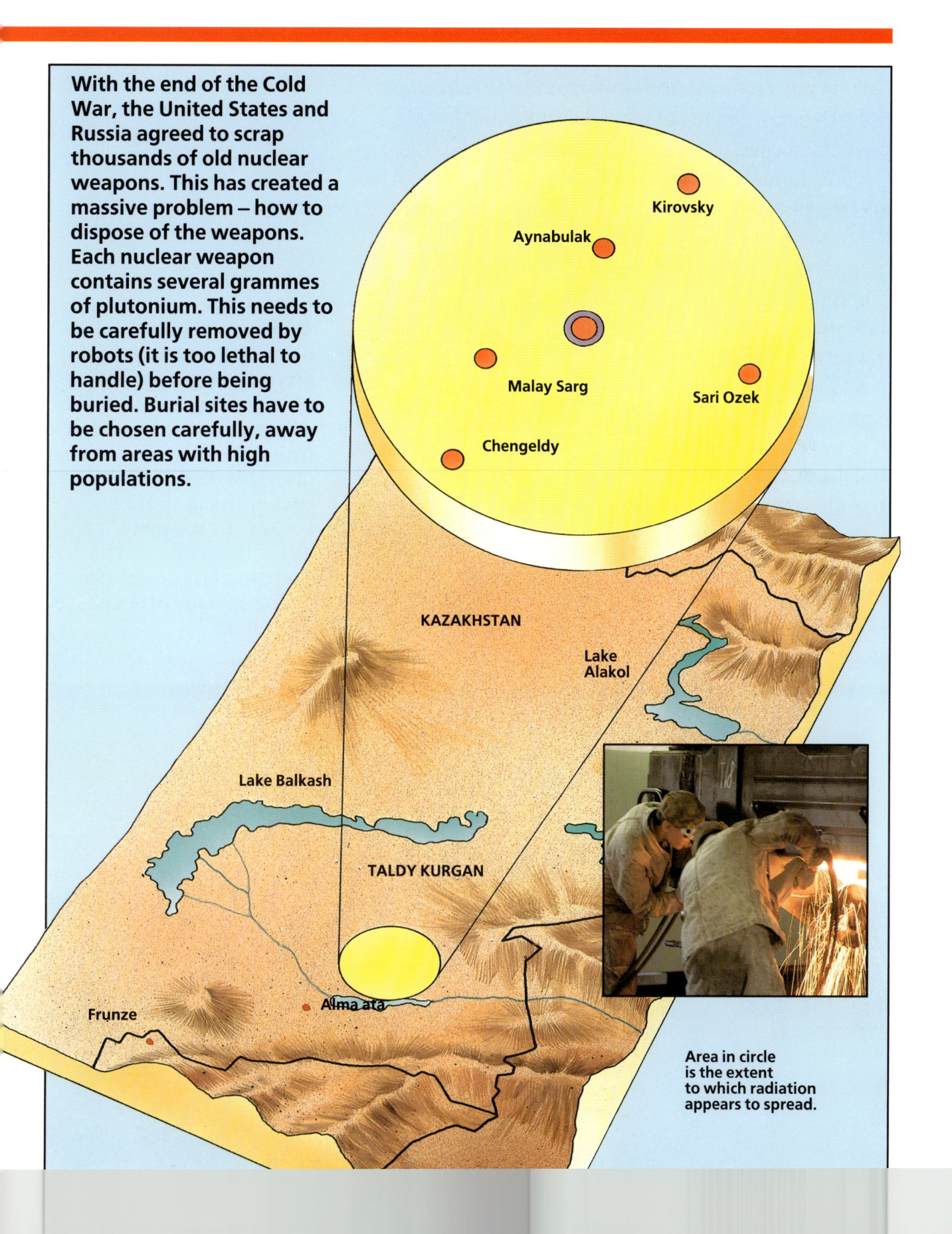

With the end of the Cold War, the United States and Russia agreed to scrap thousands of old nuclear weapons. This has created a massive problem – how to dispose of the weapons. Each nuclear weapon contains several grammes of plutonium. This needs to be carefully removed by robots (it is too lethal to handle) before being buried. Burial sites have to be chosen carefully, away from areas with high populations.

Kirovsky
Aynabulak
Malay Sarg
Sari Ozek
Chengeldy

KAZAKHSTAN
Lake Alakol
Lake Balkash
TALDY KURGAN
Frunze
Alma ata

Area in circle is the extent to which radiation appears to spread.

# REPAIRING THE LAND

Aphids are a menace to farmers and can ruin crops, but ladybirds love to eat them. Unfortunately, many pesticides used to kill the aphids also kill ladybirds. Organic farmers are developing ways of using ladybirds and other insects as a means of controlling pests.

Some countries have passed laws that require companies to deal with their toxic waste, instead of dumping it illegally on the land. Others have asked their industries to produce less wastes during the manufacturing process.

A lot of poisons in the soil end up entering the water supply. A new method of breaking down these poisons is being developed in America using the sun's rays. The sun breaks down the poisonous chemicals in the water and turns them into less harmful substances.

Crop rotation is another way of reducing damage to the soil. The different crops add nutrients and keep the soil healthy. This reduces the need for artificial fertilizers which strip the soil of its natural goodness.

▼ People cleaning up the beach in Brittany, France, after an oil spillage. Oil spillages leave a black, sticky mess along beach fronts. The beaches become unusable, and once the oil gets onto the clothes or bodies of swimmers, it is difficult to remove. The company responsible for the oil spillage often has to clean it up.

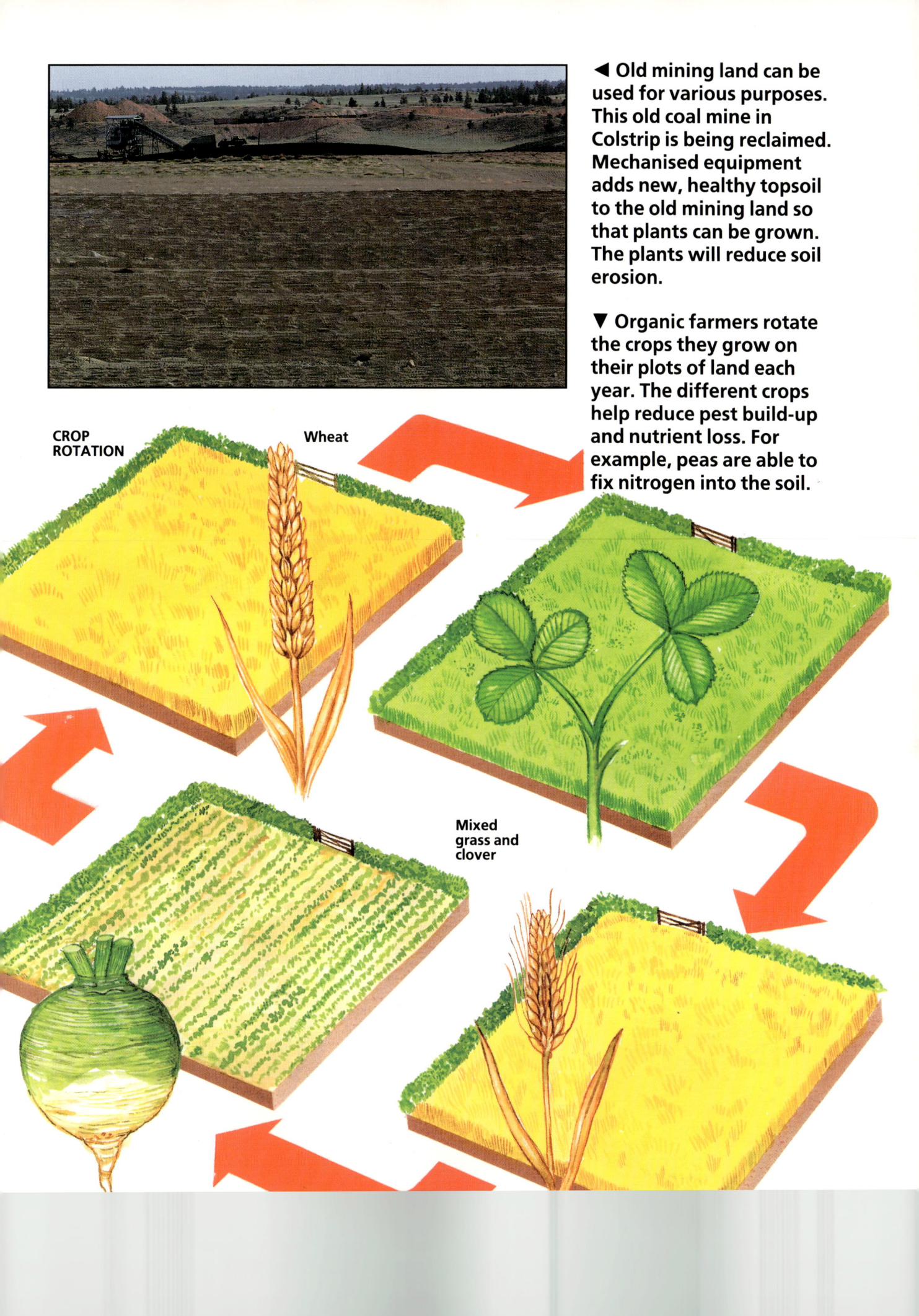

◀ Old mining land can be used for various purposes. This old coal mine in Colstrip is being reclaimed. Mechanised equipment adds new, healthy topsoil to the old mining land so that plants can be grown. The plants will reduce soil erosion.

▼ Organic farmers rotate the crops they grow on their plots of land each year. The different crops help reduce pest build-up and nutrient loss. For example, peas are able to fix nitrogen into the soil.

**CROP ROTATION**

Wheat

Mixed grass and clover

# WHAT CAN BE DONE

Large chemical companies have discovered that they can save millions of pounds by introducing schemes which prevent pollution. For example, some companies no longer bleach paper to make it white. Therefore, they do not have to spend large sums of money disposing of the poisonous by-product – dioxin.

In Britain, 18 per cent of electricity is produced by nuclear plants. But other methods of producing electricity are being developed, such as harnessing wave energy. The windy coastline of Britain is an ideal location for hundreds of wind farms, which could be used to generate electricity.

In coal-burning power stations, adding limestone (calcium carbonate) to the furnaces can prevent poisonous gases from escaping into the atmosphere. The process also produces a useful by-product called gypsum. Gypsum is used in the building industry.

People could recycle more of their rubbish, and solar power could be used to drive cars instead of petrol. Solar-powered cars turn the sun's energy into electricity.

▼ **A wind farm at South Point in Hawaii. Wind farms can be used as an alternative source of energy. The blades of the wind turbine travel faster than the wind, and can be used to generate electricity. Wind farms can provide all the power needed for lights and other home appliances.**

A plant used to recycle domestic and industrial wastes. Many of the things we throw away as rubbish – aluminium cans, bottles and paper – can be collected and taken to special sites to be recycled. A lot of old car parts are re-used by the motor car industry.

# WHAT YOU CAN DO

There are many ways you can help save the land from pollution. Using products which can be recycled, such as milk bottles, will help get rid of a lot of litter. You could also re-use all the plastic carrier bags from the supermarket. Another way of helping would be to save all your old newspapers. Some of them could be used with rotting vegetables to make compost. The rest could be recycled to produce new paper. Try and buy organically-grown food where possible, and use paper which has been recycled.

## Useful addresses:

**Friends of the Earth**
26-28 Underwood Street
London N1 7JQ
*Tel 071-490 1555*

**Greenpeace**
Canonbury Villas
London N1 2PN
*Tel 071 354-5100*

**Soil Association**
86 Colston Street
Bristol BS1 5BB
*Tel 0272 290 661*

**The Environment Council**
80 York Way
London N1 9AG
*Tel 071 278 4736*

**DESIGNING A POSTER:**
One of the most important things that can be done is to make more people aware of land pollution. One way you can do this is to make a poster to hang up at school.
(1) Think up a striking and clever heading for the poster which will grab the attention of the viewers.
(2) Design an illustration or symbol like the one shown on the opposite page. You can cut pictures out of a magazine or make a montage to convey a theme.
(3) Read through this book and try to summarise in about 40 words why poisoning the land is a threat to all living things.
(4) Make some suggestions as to how we can solve the problem of land poisoning.
(5) Include some other information if there is room, such as addresses to contact.

# THERE'S A SOLUTION TO OUR POLLUTION

OUR VALUABLE LAND IS BEING POISONED AND DESTROYED BY OVER FARMING, DUMPING OF WASTE, RADIOACTIVITY, AND POISONS INDUSTRY PRODUCE EVERY DAY. SOON THERE WILL BE LITTLE USEFUL LAND LEFT.

WHAT CAN YOU DO?
- BUY ORGANIC PRODUCE TO REDUCE THE USE OF FERTILIZERS.
- TRY GROWING YOUR OWN VEGETABLES IN YOUR OWN ORGANIC GARDEN.
- RECYCLE AS MUCH AS YOU CAN TO REDUCE HOUSEHOLD WASTE.
- DISPOSE

USEFUL ADDRESSES

# FACT FILE 1

**Gruinard Island**
Gruinard, an island off the coast of Scotland, was used to test biological bombs during World War Two. The bombs were to be Britain's weapon of mass destruction, an answer to the Japanese who had already started using germ warfare against the Chinese. The scientists tested the bomb on sheep, and within a few days they were all dead. The island is now contaminated with anthrax spores and no one is allowed to live there. A sign put up by the British government on the shore warns people of the dangers of entering the island. The sign reads:

"Gruinard Island, this island is government property under experiment. The ground is contaminated with anthrax and is dangerous. Landing is prohibited."

**Housing the People**
Areas of land that have been ruined by man's activities, such as mining or deforestation, can sometimes be put to good use. As long as the area does not contain harmful radiation or poisonous chemicals, it can support plant and animal life. The land in the picture above has been used to build homes for people to live in, hence solving yet another problem of man – homelessness.

Many homes can be built on this site, and with careful planting schemes, crops and flowers can be made to grow.

Not all reclaimed land is used for housing. Sometimes, the land is used to build schools or hospitals. At other times, it may be left lying fallow and could turn into a wasteland.

Land recovered from mines can be used for such useful things as farms. This is much more difficult as the unhealthy, weak soil has to be treated until it can support plant life again. Some people dig up the topsoil and replace it with much richer soil from other areas. This speeds up soil rejuvination and helps protect it from erosion.

### A new golf course

Unsightly rubbish tips do not have to be around for years, polluting the land and atmosphere. They can be turned into useful lands. This golf course at Settler's Hill in America was built over a huge garbage dump. First of all, the rubbish was taken away to be burnt at an incinerator. Then beans and clovers were planted to put some nutrients back into the damaged soil. Once the soil became more fertile, it was able to support grasses and other shrubs. The land is much more useful, and more environmentally-friendly, as a golf course than as a rubbish tip.

### Hong Kong

The picture below shows a view of Hong Kong taken from Victoria Peak. Six million people live and work in Hong Kong, an extremely polluted area. Everyday, two million tonnes of sewage and industrial waste are produced by people living in Hong Kong. Half of the sewage is dumped untreated into the ocean. Out of the 42 beaches in Hong Kong, only 16 are fit for bathing. The surrounding seabed is full of toxic mud containing poisonous metals such as chromium, cadmium and copper because of uncontrolled dumping. The waste dumped in the ocean creates a poisonous "red tide" of algae on the beaches, and shellfish are too toxic to eat. However, industrial growth is still encouraged in the city despite the high cost to the environment.

# FACT FILE 2

Seveso is a town in Italy which had a large chemical factory. In 1976, the factory exploded and over 18 square kilometres of land was contaminated with a toxic substance called dioxin. Nine hundred people had to be evacuated from the the town. The immediate effect of the dioxin pollution was very unpleasant. People developed a skin disease called chloracne, but scientists feared that the residents of Seveso would suffer for years afterwards. Two years after the explosion, the number of deformed babies born in the area was eighteen times higher than normal. However, doctors admit that no proper records were kept before the incident so the figures might be misleading. What is known for certain is that mice and rats that come into contact with dioxins give birth to deformed babies. Dioxin is not deliberately manufactured by industries but is a waste product produced when substances containing chlorine are incinerated. Burning PVC plastics in gardens can also produce dioxins. Some farms which are situated near incineration plants where plastics are burnt have had to destroy their cow's milk because it became contaminated with dioxins.

# GLOSSARY

**Acid rain** – rain which is made acidic when pollution from industrial areas and cars reacts with water in the atmosphere. It can damage trees and soil and can acidify lakes.

**Crop rotation** – a farming method wherby crops grown on a field are rotated from year to year.

**Deforestation** – the unrestricted logging of forests which have turned many tropical and temperate forests into wastelands, destroying trees and thousands of animal, bird and insect species.

**Desertification** – the process by which dry lands turn to deserts. This can be caused by overgrazing of cattle. Also excessive farming reduces soil fertility and can lead to desertification.

**Dioxin** – the name for a group of similar substances which are produced when chlorine is incinerated. Dioxins are considered highly toxic and are thought to cause cancer in humans.

**Erosion** – the washing or blowing away of the soil by the wind or rain.

**Fertilizer** – substance containing chemicals used to make plants grow.

**Food chain** – The links between living things that depend on each other for their food.

**Incineration** – the burning of domestic and industrial wastes at very high temperatures.

**Landfill** – an area of land where rubbish is buried in the soil. Most domestic rubbish and industrial waste is dumped at landfill sites.

**Nitrates** – main ingredient in fertilizers which farmers use to boost their crop yield.

**Organic farming** – farming which uses only natural substances like manure to grow crops.

**Pesticides** – chemicals which are used to kill insects, other plant pests and weeds.

**PVC** – (polyvinyl chloride) a plastic made from chlorine.

**Recycling** – reclaiming the useful materials from waste so that they can be used again.

**Solvents** – liquids made from hydrogen, carbon and chlorine which dry very quickly, and are often toxic.

# INDEX

**A**
acid rain 5, 12, 18, 19, 31
air pollution 5, 12, 16, 18, 19

**B**
biological weapons 28

**C**
cancer 5, 9, 12, 14, 20
chlorine 18, 30
copper mines 12, 13
crop rotation 22, 23, 31

**D**
deforestation 8, 11, 31
desertification 10, 31
dioxins 18, 24, 30, 31
domestic waste 16, 17

**E**
electricity 20, 24
energy sources 5, 24
erosion 6, 8, 13, 23, 28, 31

**F**
farming 7, 8-9, 10, 11, 22, 23, 28
fertilizers 5, 8, 9, 10, 22, 31
food chain 5, 7, 14, 18, 20, 31
fossil fuels 19, 24

**G**
Gruinard Island 28

gypsum 24

**H**
herbicides 9
Hong Kong 17, 29
housing 28

**I**
incineration 30, 31

**L**
land use 11, 23, 28, 29
landfill sites 14, 20, 31
lead 12, 18
logging 11

**M**
methane 17
mines 12, 13, 20, 23, 28

**N**
nitrates 23, 31
nuclear waste 5, 20-1

**O**
oil 13, 14
oil spillages 16, 22
organic farming 9, 10, 22, 23, 31
ozone layer 17

**P**
pesticides 5, 8, 9, 14, 22, 31
photosynthesis 6
plant life 5, 6, 7, 9, 20

power plants 18, 20, 24
PVC plastics 18, 30, 31

**R**
radioactive pollution 20-1
radon gas 12, 20
rainforests 6, 11
recycling 5, 24, 25, 26, 31

**S**
Seveso 30
sewage 16, 29
soil 6, 7, 8, 10, 19
soil pollution 5, 12, 14, 19, 20, 30
solar power 24
solvents 14, 31
subsoil 6
subsurface mining 13
surface mining 13

**T**
topsoil 6, 8, 23, 28
toxic wastes 5, 14-15, 18, 22, 29
tree planting schemes 10, 11

**U**
uranium 12, 20

**W**
water pollution 16, 22, 29
wind farms 24

**Photographic Credits:**
Cover and pages 7, 11, 13 top, 15 middle top and 28: Spectrum Colour Library; pages 4-5, 15 bottom, 18, 29 top and 30: Frank Spooner Pictures; pages 8, 9, 12-13, 14, 20-21 and 22: Science Photo Library; pages 12, 15 top and 29 bottom: Eye Ubiquitous; pages 13 bottom, 16-17, 19 and 21: The Hutchison Library; pages 15 middle left and 16: NHPA; pages 15 middle right and 24: Robert Harding Picture Libary; page 23: Bruce Coleman Limited; page 25: Jonathon Eastland.